How to u~~...~~s

Guided Rea

Walkthrough/Book introduction *(pages 2–5)*

A *walkthrough* or book introduction is a way of introducing the book to a group of children. It provides an opportunity to introduce children to some of the ideas and words they will meet when they read the book.

Go through the whole book in the walkthrough, before children start reading independently. The walkthrough notes on pages 2 to 5 of this booklet provide prompts for you to use. These will alert children to the ideas and vocabulary they will need when they come to read the book for themselves.

Independent Reading *(pages 2–5)*

After doing a walkthrough of the whole book, ask the children to read the text aloud, on their own, at their own pace. Observe each child, praising successful strategies and expressive reading.

The Independent Reading notes on pages 2 to 5 of this booklet offer suggestions for prompting children to check, correct and confirm their own reading.

After Independent Reading/Returning to the text *(page 6)*

After the children have read the book independently, return to the text as a group, to reinforce teaching points and check children's understanding. On page 6 there are quick follow-up ideas for related text, sentence and word level work.

Responding to the text *(pages 6–8)*

It is important to encourage children to give a personal response to the text. Discussion ideas related to the book are given on page 6.

These Teaching Notes also contain group activity ideas on page 7 and a Photocopy Master on page 8, for use after the guided reading session or in a follow-up literacy session.

Guided Reading Notes

Walkthrough *(front and back cover)*

Ask the children whether they have ever visited a farm. What animals might the children expect to find in this book?

Read the title and the back cover blurb to the children.

Walkthrough *(title page)*

PROMPTS Do you remember the title? Let's say it together.

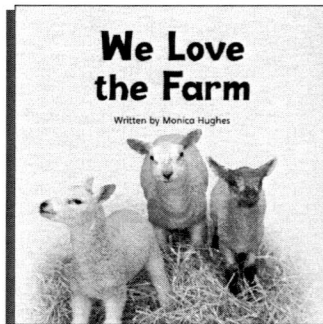

Independent Reading *(title page)*

CHECK that the child is using one-to-one correspondence.

"Did your pointing fit? I liked the way you pointed carefully without covering the words."

Walkthrough *(pages 2–3)*

PROMPTS What is this boy doing? Yes, he says, *Look at me driving a tractor.* Do you think he loves tractors? Let's all say what the boy says: *I love tractors.*

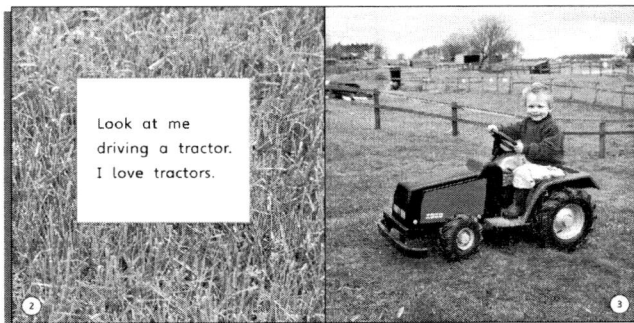

Look at me
driving a tractor.
I love tractors.

Independent Reading *(pages 2–3)*

CHECK that the child is following the direction of the print, and making the return sweep.

"I liked the way your finger went back to the beginning of each new line."

Walkthrough *(pages 4–5)*

PROMPTS What is this boy doing? What do you think he is saying to us? Yes, *Look at me feeding a lamb.* Do you think he loves lambs? What does he say? Yes, he says, *I love lambs.*

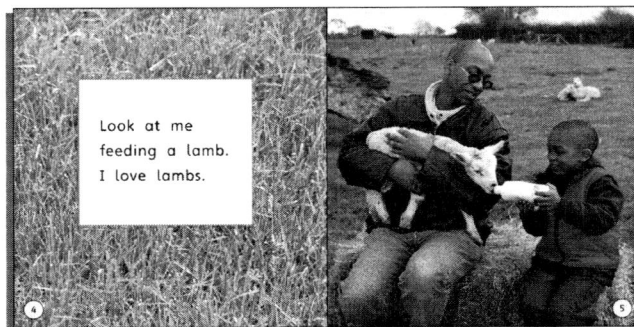

Look at me
feeding a lamb.
I love lambs.

Independent Reading *(pages 4–5)*

CHECK that the child is using initial sound clues.

"How did you know that word said *feeding*? Yes, that's right, it starts with *f*."

Walkthrough *(pages 6–7)*

PROMPTS What do you think this girl is saying? Does she love rabbits? What does she say?

> Look at me
> holding a rabbit.
> I love rabbits.

Independent Reading *(pages 6–7)*

CHECK that the child has recognized the text pattern.

"Well done. You've noticed the words have a pattern. I can hear it in your reading."

Walkthrough *(pages 8–9)*

PROMPTS What is this boy doing? Yes, he's patting a horse. What do you think he is saying to us?

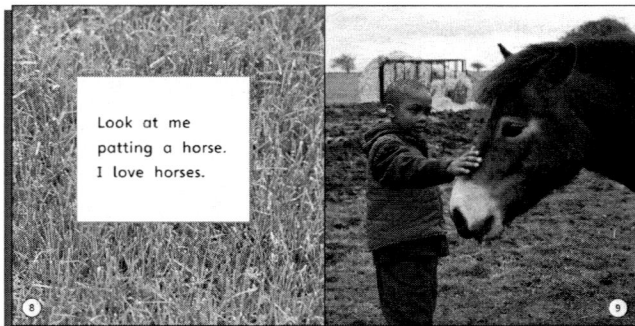

> Look at me
> patting a horse.
> I love horses.

Independent Reading *(pages 8–9)*

CHECK for accurate reading of the word *patting*.

If the child says *stroking* … "You read *stroking*. If it was *stroking*, what would the first sound of the word be? Look at the first sound. Does that help you sort it out?"

Walkthrough *(pages 10–11)*

PROMPTS What do you think is in the bucket? Yes, food for the hens. What do you think the girl is saying?

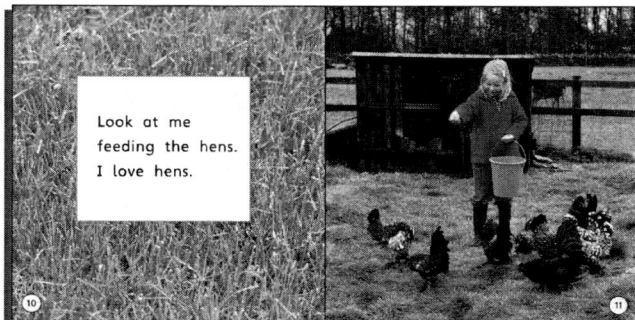

> Look at me
> feeding the hens.
> I love hens.

Independent Reading *(pages 10–11)*

CHECK that the child reads with expression.

"I liked the way you read this, it sounded just like talking."

Walkthrough *(page 12)*

PROMPTS Now the children are all together. What are they holding? What might they be saying?

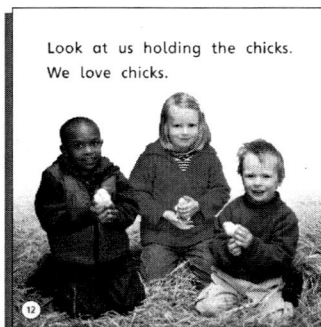

> Look at us holding the chicks.
> We love chicks.

Independent Reading *(page 12)*

CHECK that the child has noticed the change from *me* to *us*.

"Well done. You noticed that they are all talking together. How did you know it said *us*?" (Prompt for change in initial sound and more than one child being in the picture.)

After Independent Reading/Returning to the text

Word knowledge – *L/l*
Locate and compare the capital and lower case *L/l* in the words *Look* and *love* on page 4. Can the children find any other *L/l* words in the book? (Make sure the children include the capital *L* on the cover and title page.)

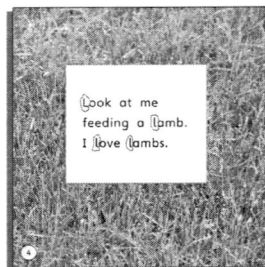

Look at me
feeding a lamb.
I love lambs.

Text knowledge – expressive reading
Ask the children to reread the text, making sure that they read the second sentence on each page with extra enthusiasm, so it sounds as if someone is talking.

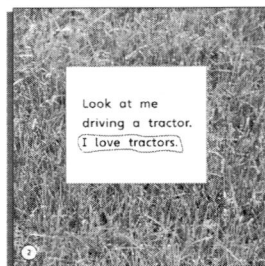

Look at me
driving a tractor.
I love tractors.

Text knowledge – recounts
This is a very simple example of a common non-fiction text type – a recount. If you have been working on other non-fiction recounts, look at some of the differences and similarities between this and other recounts the children have read, e.g. compare tenses. (This text is written in the present tense, but often recounts are written in the past tense.) It may be appropriate on a second or subsequent reading to look at the index inside the back cover, but do not tackle this on a first reading with children at this stage of reading development.

Index
chicks 12
hens 10
horse 8
lamb 4
rabbit 6
tractor 2

Responding to the text
● Have any of the children ever visited a farm? What did they see and do?
● Which of the animals and machinery featured in the book do they like the best?

① L/l

AIM to identify the initial letter *l* and match it to pictures or artefacts (NLS: YR W2)

YOU WILL NEED
- a bag of objects beginning with *l* with which the children are familiar, e.g. a letter/lemon/leaf/lollipop, etc, and some objects beginning with other initial letters
- board, flip chart or magnetic board
- marker pen or magnetic letters

WHAT TO DO Ask the children to take it in turns to take an object out of the bag. If the object begins with *l*, the child puts a magnetic letter *l* on the magnetic board or writes an *l* on the board/flip chart. Discuss other things in the classroom starting with *l* that the children could put in the bag.

The children might want to bring in objects from home to add to the collection.

② Word making

AIM to consolidate learning of high frequency words *a/at/me/we/the/look* and adding *s* to make plural words (NLS: YR W2, 6)

YOU WILL NEED ● magnetic board and letters, or letter cards

WHAT TO DO Give each child in the group the following letters: *a/e/h/k/l/m/oo/w/t*. In pairs or individually, ask the children to make high frequency words when they are called out. The words can be built up by adding or replacing letters, e.g. start with the letter *a*, then make it into *at*. Start with *me*, then change it to *we*. Can some children change the letters from *look* to make *book* and *took*?

When the children are confident with their word making, they could try adding *s* to make plural words, e.g. changing the word *chick* to *chicks*.

PCM — Farmyard map

 tractor  lambs 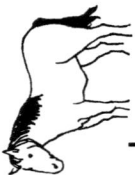 horse  rabbit  chicks

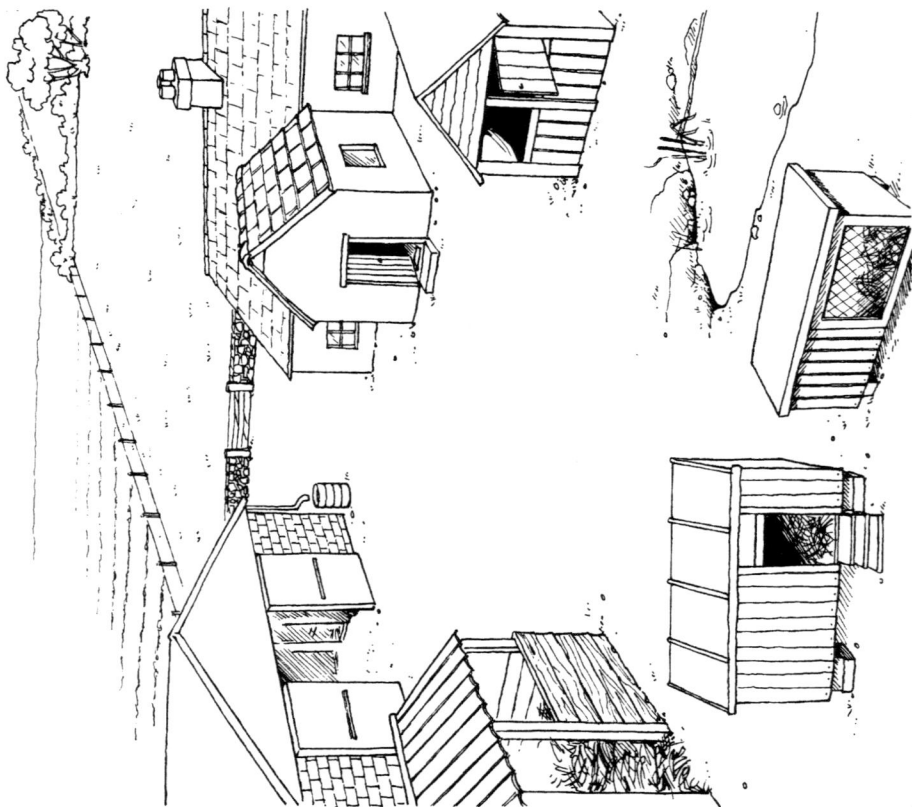

This is a group activity but could be adapted for individual or paired work.
Enlarge the PCM farmyard picture preferably to A3 size. Cut out the labelled items and ask the children to read the words. Discuss where each item could be placed on the farmyard map. The children could then complete their own farmyard using their own PCM and use it for storytelling or as a base for playing with 3D farmyard animals.

We Love the Farm   *(NLS: YR W2; T1)*